# YES FIRST

# YES FIRST

LIVE CONSCIOUS AND CAREFREE

# TAKING ACTION

AS A WAY OF LIFE

# IN UNCERTAIN TIMES

WRITTEN BY

## STEFANIE DUMONT

CONSCIOUS & CAREFREE
CARDIFF-BY-THE-SEA, CA

Editors: Christine McDowell Hayden and Bennett Lewis
Interior Design and Consultant: Tanya Brockett, HallagenInk.com

Ordering Information:
Special discounts may be available on large purchases by corporations, associations, book clubs, event planners, and others. For details, email ConsciousCarefree@gmail.com.

Yes First / Stefanie Dumont—1st ed.

*This first volume is dedicated to my beloved husband Bennett Lewis, my behind-the-scenes editor, snuggler, and creative genius. Making the big book, and now the first mini book alongside you is a divine partnership dream come true and kept my heart on my vision. I am deeply grateful for your love, guidance, and support.*

# Contents

Foreword.................................................................ix

Introduction .........................................................xi

Ask For What You Want.......................................1

Summoning Greater Love ....................................9

Befriending Uncertainty ....................................15

Saying Yes, First.................................................23

Finding Your Zone .............................................31

About the Author................................................39

Free Gift..............................................................41

# Foreword

Stefanie is a treasure for our world because she embodies saying, "Yes" first by living Conscious and Carefree.

I first met Stefanie in 2018, while having a blast at a mutual friend's birthday party.

Upon recognizing me, she walked straight over to the seat next to me, gently took my hand in hers, looked tenderly into my eyes, and said, "Boy, do I have a story for you! I've waited to meet you my whole life. I was thirteen years old when I attended your anti-bullying assembly at my middle school. You honored me with a 'Who I Am Makes A Difference'® Blue Ribbon, and told me that someday I would become a great leader. That moment changed my life forever."

We both realized we had come full circle, and knew we were in the right place, because life had brought us back to each other again.

Since that day, Stefanie and I have become great friends and co-mentors. We take long walks on the beach, share successes, discuss our challenges, and help one another see the light at the end of the tunnel. Every page in *Yes First* is a gentle blueprint for soul evolution.

Stefanie propels us to a place in which we feel simple bliss, clarity, and the joy of moving forward, never again being stuck in the past, not knowing who we are, or why we were born, and the difference we make. Conscious and Carefree is who she is, because she is.

Love, Grandma Sparky

*Helice "Grandma Sparky" Bridges is the founder of Blue Ribbons Worldwide, First Lady of Acknowledgement, and the creator of the "Who I Am Makes A Difference"® Blue Ribbon Acknowledgement Ceremony. Her blue-ribbon message has impacted over fifty million people worldwide and is translated into twelve languages. Grandma Sparky is a mentor to leaders of leaders teaching children and adults throughout the world how to live, dream, and succeed. She is the heart of community building.*

# Introduction

*What if everything you learned about how to
succeed in life didn't apply anymore?*

*What if you actually had the answers, and all you
needed was someone to ask you the right
questions?*

*Yes First, Taking Action in Uncertain Times* is
the first volume in a series of coaching guidebooks
for moving forward in joy. Uncertainty has become
part of life, the only thing in our control is ourselves.
In order to experience consistent fulfillment, it is
essential to tune in to who we are now and do a deep
dive into what each of us require to take action. This
is your invitation to point your canoe downstream
and ride the current. It's all here and I'll be your
behind-the-scenes coach on this journey.

While a book isn't really a substitute for a professional
coach or a mastermind group, this first volume is

designed for you to achieve similar results. To get where you're going next requires accountability. You don't need to figure it all out on your own anymore; you'll have a co-pilot with you. You don't have to wait until you can see the whole picture; you're creating in real time now. Say yes first, and experience what happens next!

Over the years of my obsession with optimal performance, and leading-edge thought, the answer I have found is living Conscious and Carefree. In fact, it's the secret sauce to a consistently happy, big, and meaningfully productive life. My clients who live Conscious and Carefree, lead better, love more, act larger, find flow, serve with contribution, and enjoy adventure. Want in? Of course you do!

I'm thrilled to have you, because my vision is a community of leaders and visionary game changers looking to collaborate and make things better while they build their legacy. Only those who walk their talk need apply. In the past, people believed you could only live one way and not the other, but you'll soon find living both Conscious and Carefree is the way.

As you go through each chapter in this book, you will experience aha moments you want to collect—have a pen and notebook handy. At the end of each chapter, the magic begins: you will answer three powerful questions that will lead you to extract your own insight, and take you straight into action. For best results with this book, follow through and take the action immediately after you read the chapter.

Once you complete this entire book, you will:

- Feel ready for what's next and experience greater confidence and clarity;

- Suddenly notice a paradigm shift on how to move forward with essential areas in your personal and professional life;

- Stay in action with greater love, finding daily flow, going straight to solution, feeling comfortable in uncertainty, and moving forward without the whole picture.

After reading *Yes First*, you'll be ready for Volume Two, which you can request at: bcarefree.com. But right now, we will take it one step at a time.

I look forward to seeing you at the end of this short journey. Now, let's get to it!

XO,

Stefanie

*"You get in life what you have the courage to ask for."*

—OPRAH WINFREY

# Ask For What You Want

I was working with a Pilates instructor recently, and she said that she didn't feel good. She was not aware of it, but she was saying it repeatedly. It was a mental complaint, not a physical one. I thought to myself, Does she realize that you get what you ask for?

When we affirm something negative in thought or language, it unconsciously repeats itself in our minds over and over again. If we understand the power of repetition, why wouldn't we practice right thought and communication as adults? What keeps us from right speech or affirming what we want?

## What are you thinking?

If we were corrected with negativity as a child, we have a tendency to tell ourselves negative statements as adults. Negativity in thought and speech is a learned habit or pattern. Unless we consciously change our thoughts and language to what we want, it is conceivable that we will continue to have what we say we don't want. This has been referred to as the Law of Attraction. The Law of Attraction states that you will attract more of what you are thinking, saying, and feeling. The more you think about something, the more you talk about it, and the more you talk about something, the more you bring it about; it starts with what we're thinking!

## Negativity is the norm

As a society we are taught to complain about things that are not to our liking, instead of asking for what we want. Unfortunately, most people don't know what they want. If someone is feverishly complaining about something and you ask them what they want, many people will have a difficult time answering. On the other hand, if you ask someone what makes them miserable, they will answer you immediately with a list of twenty things.

Have you noticed that? If you ask what makes them happy, they will pause and say, "Uh, I don't know." In order for us to ask clearly for what we want, we need to become more aware of the things that make us feel good.

## Seeking solutions

I use the act of complaining, especially a reoccurring complaint, as a call to action. Why would I continue to harp on a negative circumstance without resolving it? What a waste of energy! Not resolving an issue takes up space in my brain.

In the coaching world we call this phenomenon a "toleration." A toleration is an unresolved thing or issue that causes us to have a negative reaction. A toleration could be a check engine light that comes on each time you start your car, or kitchen blinds that come loose each time you close them at night. It could also be an unresolved conflict with a friend.

My goal is to live toleration free and to teach my clients to do the same, as this breeds a great deal of fulfillment. When people have nothing to complain about, they can move forward at a steady pace, and life is much sweeter. It's not that you never complain about something, it's that if you do talk about it, you seek a solution or resolution of what you would like to have happen. You don't incessantly repeat the story of the problem.

**Be specific**

The game changer here is a reminder to ask for what you want. Be specific! The people around you will appreciate it, because they won't feel like they have to guess, walk around on eggshells, or disappoint you.

Watch your thoughts like a hawk. If you harp on about what you don't want, correct yourself with what you would like instead. Be vocal about it, be courageous, be willing to get a little uncomfortable if necessary...this is what leads us to our greatest growth. And who doesn't want to grow? Because if we're not busy living, we're busy transitioning out. Let's use our time here wisely. Let's do all we can. Practice asking for what you want. When you see the tides turning because of your courage, and manifest things you only dreamed of, you'll be very happy you did!

## *Insight*

*What's one thing you find yourself complaining a lot about lately?*

*What is a positive thing you would like to happen instead?*

*What is one courageous thing you can do this week to practice asking for what you want?*

## *Action*

*Make the call now and ask for it.*

*"You don't need to justify your love, you don't need to explain your love, you just need to practice your love. Practice creates the master."*

—DON MIGUEL RUIZ

# Summoning Greater Love

Love is evolving, just like we are. What was important one year ago might be completely irrelevant in your life now. If COVID has taught us anything, it has taught us that what is precious in life: family, relationships, and connection. How we related to each other before the great pause is likely different than how we find ourselves relating now. At least it is for me. I am reaching out more, making deeper connections, and interestingly, with different people. I am spending more quality time with my family, one, because they are here, and two, because they need more hands-on nurturing and support. Heck, I need more hands-on nurturing and support!

I'm learning to ask for it, and to ask for what I need now, today, with friends and family, and now to my readers, in a way I never have before. I want to increase my level of intimacy with my husband and get to know who he is today, what's most important to him now, and what he might need from me that he hasn't up until this point.

I want to summon more love for myself, by giving more to myself, by asking myself what I need in this moment; not just when I break down, but on an ordinary day. Although it seems there are no more ordinary days, because we are now living or getting used to living in an extraordinary time. No matter how we normalize this time, it is different and new. I am different and new. With regard to love, what could be more enlightening, delicious, and delightful? Nothing. Love has more meaning than it ever has. Maybe it has more meaning because we have less of an opportunity to share it now. I'm learning to express love in new ways, over Zoom, via text, sending personalized gifts, sharing encouraging daily readings and quotes, making more calls, and staying on the phone longer just to hear someone's voice.

It has never been so important for us to connect, and I value you and your readership. I still consider this exchange a dance we do together. We might not dance as often, but when we do, it is oh so sweet, and I have been waiting patiently to dance with you. Thank you for your interest, your desire to learn and grow and share what is important to you, now. All this is in greater love and the summoning of something perhaps we've never had before.

---

### Insight

*List as many places as you can where you are currently feeling love in your life.*

*List any places where you might not be experiencing much love.*

*Where is the gap? How can you invite more love into the areas where you are not experiencing much?*

## *Action*

*Act in a way you'd like others to behave. Become an example. Do something different today to summon greater love.*

*"Some things cannot be spoken or discovered until we have been stuck, incapacitated, or blown off course for a while. Plain sailing is pleasant, but you are not going to explore many unknown realms that way."*

—DAVID WHYTE

# Befriending Uncertainty

Becoming comfortable in uncertainty requires a shift in mindset and perception. In the past, we were taught it was normal to be uncomfortable throughout an entire process, until we were sure we had arrived at our destination or achieved a specific goal. How does this archaic thinking assist us in joyfully achieving our next level? It doesn't.

**Taking the first step**

We don't always know the plan or aren't always able to see the entire staircase. But you can take the first step or two, and notice things begin to unfold, sometimes in ways you were unable to imagine initially. People often stall until they have the big picture or until they feel ready to make the big jump. It's like having a baby...is anyone ever fully prepared? You can wait your entire life to make that leap toward your next level if you don't summon the courage and confidence to take that first step today.

## Know how you'd like to feel

We don't always know the right decisions to make or exactly what to do in a situation, but often we can identify how we want to feel. When we were planning our wedding several years ago, we had a lot of decisions to make. At the beginning of planning, a dear friend stepped in as a surrogate mother and lovingly took my calls regarding big decisions. Whenever I would ask her what to do, she would turn it around and ask me, "How do you want your day to feel?" That was a question I could readily answer, as it took me from my head straight to my heart. As capable as our minds are, we need to begin making more decisions from the heart. Our head gets overwhelmed, confused, and blocked, while our hearts hold pure knowledge and clarity. When in doubt, ask your heart.

## The way we've always done things does not necessarily work today

Knowing who you are and defining your strengths has become a standard to succeed in this world. In the face of uncertainty, we need something, someone, we can rely on. That someone is us. A favorite coaching client came to a stunning conclusion after feeling devastated by her acclaimed role model, and realized it was time to step into her mentoring shoes. No one was going to do what my client knew needed to be done, or in a way only she knew how to do it. I remember clearly when my client spoke the words aloud on our call, "I am the one I've been waiting for!"

Building our awareness and self-knowledge defeats difficulty and befriends uncertainty. It's not just about what we do anymore; a large part of our trajectory and success is coming from who we are. We will achieve only what we think we can, nothing more.

## It's time to change the dialogue

Have conversations with people about what you'd like to have happen (create solutions vs. focus on problems). An old boss of mine required us to present him with three solutions to any problem we brought to complain about. It was an effective method, and forced his staff to focus on what they wanted instead of what they weren't getting. You cannot solve a problem with the same thinking that got you there. New circumstances and opportunities require new perception, new thinking, new language, and new action. One of my favorite quotes that sits on top of my bookshelf is, "If you want something you never had, you have to do something you've never done." And I'll add...you must be someone you've never been.

## Fear vs. love

You can't simultaneously have both fear and love, similar to poverty vs. wealth. You are focused on one or the other. Your mind cannot hold a positive thought and a negative thought simultaneously, it's this one or that one, you choose. If you want to champion yourself to new heights, if you want a better country or a better world, be clear...it starts with you. Fear is a control mechanism of the past; let's give it the boot once and for all, so we can go higher than ever before. If we focus on love, compassion, and self-care, fear doesn't have a chance...and uncertainty will be something we gently put our arm around as we stroll down the path of life.

---

### Insight

*List three things you are uncertain about.*

*Recall a time when you had significant uncertainty before you succeeded, but were ultimately successful. What happened? How did it feel? What helped you?*

*What can you learn from your past success that can help you navigate uncertainty in the three areas you listed above?*

### Action

*Pick one area you would like to move forward on now. Take the first step.*

*"If somebody offers you an amazing opportunity but you are not sure you can do it, say yes—then learn how to do it later!"*

—RICHARD BRANSON

# Saying Yes,
# First

I was helping my son figure out his next steps in life. He shared how happy he was about where he is and how much he's enjoying his life. This was music to my ears. As a few quiet tears ran down his face, he stated he was not sure if he was ready to leave for college in the fall, that it might be too soon for him, and he realized he had not yet settled on the college of his dreams. He received his first acceptance, so it wasn't a matter of not getting in. I feel for him. I'm not sure who decided at the age of eighteen we are adults who are supposed to go away from our home, friends, and loved ones, live by ourselves, and all of a sudden figure life out on our own. Getting to know ourselves takes time.

Even as adults, we are often unsure about what steps to take or what territory to explore next. Sometimes we don't have a grand plan and we're unsure of the next juncture in our lives. I explained to my son that this is quite normal, especially at his age, but I also explained to him that much of life is this way; the road sign ahead is not always a bright green light telling you when to go or which way to turn. I told him the greatest things that have occurred for me thus far happened before I thought I was ready. I said yes first, before knowing what to do with it. One of my favorite quotes, which still rules the day, is "my life is a performance of which I have yet to rehearse." Much of my life has been the act of jumping without yet being able to see the net. Or being thrown into a pool, without first being taught to swim. Have you felt this?

When I look back, I realize that trusting myself is how I have gotten where I am. Saying yes first is how I've up-leveled before and continue to do so today. I explained to my son, for me, life unfolded one opportunity at a time. When I felt strongly about one decision, it turned into the next, and the next. I followed a chain reaction of gut instincts over time, gentle tugs on my heart strings, whispers to follow my passion, to take the road less traveled, and help others do the same. We're invited to go in certain directions in our lives. Our priority is to be present with both feet on the ground and pay attention.

I have always been drawn to peak performance. Since the age of fifteen, I have been fascinated by self-esteem and communication. I had no idea what I would do with those topics, but always felt confident. Money did not define wealth for me, but the freedom to do what I wanted, when I wanted, was my prize. I knew I loved sociology, wanted divine partnership, wanted to raise happy children, and to live with a purpose.

Growing up, I never noticed a lot of happiness with the "American Dream." I watched both my parents work themselves to the bone, chasing the almighty dollar, exhausted, self-defeating, or suffering heart attacks, which can get in the way of enjoying your life. Everything society promoted and drove people to compete for, brought disharmony and dis-ease. This is not what life is about. The prize in life is different for each of us. Every so often we need to pause, reflect, and define what that prize is.

As we often need to do with ourselves, I reminded my son that I trust him and believe in his ability to know what is good for him. I told him we are here, and he does not need to know his entire plan up front. I reminded him how many great decisions he has already made: wise friends, an ambitious young woman he's dating, and enjoying work he loves while surrounded by caring people. I pointed out the beautiful relationships he has with his parents and siblings, and how he adores his home life. My son has relished being a water polo star, popular among peers, and to top it off... everywhere I go, people actually stop me and tell me what a fine young man he is. I find this remarkable. What more could a parent ask for?

Just like my son, we don't always see the big picture right away. But we can say yes first, with confidence, and tune into the frequencies of what is right for us in this moment. We can pay attention to the feelings and signs, and look at the amount of joy we are experiencing in our lives. Saying yes first opens opportunities and worlds that might not have appeared otherwise. Listening internally, releasing distractions, and tuning in are key. You may never get the guarantee you want or the permission you need from others to move ahead. Your best bet is to take the time to really get to know yourself, who you are today, take a deep breath...and jump!

## Insight

*When was the last time you said yes, first? How did it go?*

*How would your life be different if you said yes first?*

*What keeps you from saying yes?*

## Action

*Close your eyes and think of where you feel "yes." Pay attention, so you recognize what a "heck yes" feels like!*

*"I'm not thinking about anything when I'm climbing, which is part of the appeal. I'm focused on executing what's in front of me."*

—ALEX HONNOLD

# Finding Your Zone

I attended a think tank recently on the topic of "flow," or what some people refer to as "the zone." We discussed our fascination with professional athletes, musicians, and experts who palpably, moment by moment, create magic. Often fans identify the energy as the "it factor," when you see someone excelling in the sweet spot. Is being in the zone solely for the gifted or can we mere mortals learn the tricks of the trade?

## Going with the flow

We all have the ability to access flow, although some of us can drop in easier than others. Flow is a state of being; an environment where one loses track of time and space. It is a state where brilliance is born. Flow begins at the point of concentration. Flow occurs in the midst of a shower or while communing with nature. We experience flow racing our bike downhill, with wind blowing in our face. Looking back, while singing professionally at a young age, I now understand that when I performed, I went into the zone. I became unaware of my surroundings, only feeling the elation of embodying the song. Each of us has a talent or gift which takes us to this place. Our most important task in life is discovering exactly what that is.

## Points of entry

A skill my mastermind members choose to acquire is how to put themselves into the zone more often. Productivity soars in the zone, along with a stream of pure effortlessness. As a writer, it helps me to identify my inspiration before sitting down to a blank page. When I hear someone say something intriguing during a conversation or a line in a movie,

I pause and capture the idea. It is much easier for me to initiate flow on a topic by which I know I have already been inspired.

One of the tips I use in accessing the zone is to take a break. I know this might sound odd. When you're engaged in an activity that is not flowing, stopping to take a walk, shifting activities, or changing your environment can reignite flow. Steve Jobs regularly sent his staff out for a day and assigned them to do anything but work. He understood the power of flow.

## Jumping hurdles

An awareness of what blocks us is equally as important as learning techniques of entry. The most common block that keeps the zone at bay is fear; fear of anything or everything. Plain and simple, fear keeps us out of flow! Think about it...whenever we go into fear or doubt, we cannot create, tap into, or achieve our level of peak performance. Flow is trust. Trust is confidence in action, that you will innately know what you are doing, and feeling the joy while doing it. Have you ever done something for the first time that you did not think you knew how to do and totally nailed it? Congratulations, you were in "the zone."

So, when was the last time you found yourself in the zone? Have you ever experienced this state before? What were you doing? How did it feel? To prime the pump, here are some cues to help drop into flow. Feel free to add your own!

- Identify music that creates laser focus
- Choose fitness or sports that draw you inward
- Explore nature
- Align goals with your values
- Do more of what you love
- Practice meditation or chanting
- Use your olfactory senses (e.g., aromatherapy candles, incense, or oil)
- Stop and change your environment
- Identify personal touchstones
- Work in an inspiring location

## Insight

*Recall a time you experienced flow. What did you accomplish?*

*List three "flow triggers" that have worked for you in the past, or ones you believe could work for you tomorrow. Be specific (e.g., listen to "Flight of the Bumblebee" by Nikolai Rimsky-Korsakov, or take a five-minute walk, or, meditate for twelve minutes.)*

## Action

*Practice your flow entry three times this week, and journal on your outcome.*

*What do some of the most successful minds of our time have in common?*

*They collaborate in mastermind groups and strategize with a professional coach.*

—CONSCIOUS & CAREFREE

# About the Author

As an Executive and Transformational Coach for twenty years, Stefanie has helped her clients' dreams become their daily lives. From gold medal-winning Olympic athletes, to philanthropy-driven CEOs, leading physicians, award-winning artists, cutting edge professionals, and philanthropreneurs; Stefanie has coached them all. She is a catalyst who leads individuals, teams, and organizations in personal and professional transformation.

Stefanie co-Founded Conscious and Carefree, at bcarefree.com, a learning forum and community dedicated to joy, contribution, and meaningful productivity. She interviews thought leaders, facilitates socialpreneurial masterminds, and contributes articles to the media about principles and techniques she has learned to live a good life.

Stefanie guest appears on news forums, television shows, podcasts, and Awake TV Network with her show *"52 Weeks to Living Conscious and Carefree,"* based on the title of her upcoming book.

Stefanie has nurtured a beautiful family and has realized human potential is her life's work. She enjoys writing articles and songs about the human experience—translating thoughts, feelings, and ideas into action.

# Free Gift

Thank you for buying this book and coming together with leaders from around the world to live Conscious and Carefree!

If you enjoyed *Yes First, Taking Action in Uncertain Times*, the first volume of Conscious and Carefree Insights, I invite you to take our assessment: "Are You Ready to Live Conscious & Carefree?"

This assessment will give you a personal score on each of the four pillars of living Conscious and Carefree and show you some of the results you can look forward to. Your pillars are the foundation for personal and professional mastery. This assessment only takes three minutes! Take the assessment here: https://bcarefree.com/iamready.

After you take the assessment, you will also be notified when the upcoming volumes are released. Volume Two is due Spring of 2022!

To get quick tips, highlights of interviews, learn about free webinars and upcoming courses, and connect with thought leaders and individuals who live Conscious and Carefree, join our Facebook group: https://facebook.com/consciousandcarefree/community.

To visit our website with hundreds of articles and motivating thought leader interviews on Mindfulness, Wellbeing, Connection, and Up-leveling, please visit https://bcarefree.com.

For those of you interested in jumping into action via masterminds and coaching, book a discovery session with Stefanie at https://bcarefree.com/coaching-masterminds/.

Stefanie is available for professional speaking, facilitating team masterminds within your organization, or piloting workshops on "Creating a

Conscious and Carefree Culture" for your staff. She can be reached at stefanie@bcarefree.com.

Made in the USA
Columbia, SC
17 November 2022